MW01137445

The Library of Small Ecosystems™

The Ecosystem of a
Milkweed Patch

Elaine Pascoe   Photography by **Dwight Kuhn**

The Rosen Publishing Group's
PowerKids Press™
New York

Published in 2003 by The Rosen Publishing Group, Inc.
29 East 21st Street, New York, NY 10010

First Edition

Editor: Nancy MacDonell Smith
Book Design: Michael J. Caroleo

Photo Credits: Photos © Dwight Kuhn.

Pascoe, Elaine.
The ecosystem of a milkweed patch / Elaine Pascoe.— 1st ed.
    p. cm. — (The library of small ecosystems)
Includes bibliographical references (p.   ).
Summary: Describes the interdependence of some of the plants and animals that can be found in a milkweed patch.
ISBN 0-8239-6309-8 (lib. bdg.)
1. Meadow ecology—Juvenile literature. 2. Milkweeds—Ecology—Juvenile literature. [1. Meadow ecology. 2.
Ecology. 3. Milkweeds.] I. Title.
QH541.5.M4 P365 2002
577.4'6—dc21
                                                2001007783

Manufactured in the United States of America

Contents

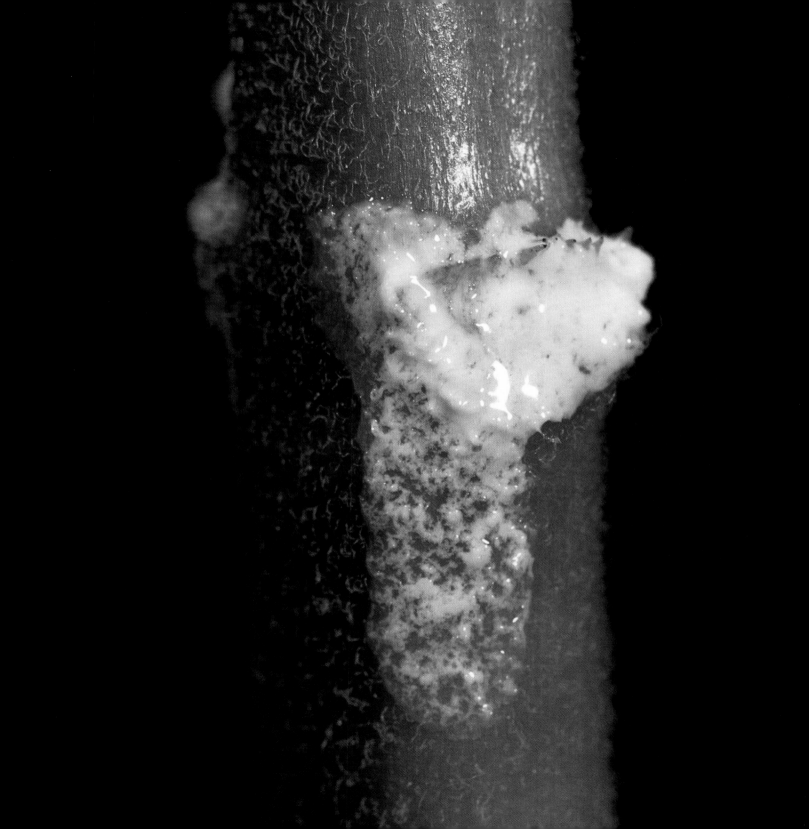

A Patch of Milkweed

A patch of milkweed may spring up almost anywhere. Common milkweed grows wild in fields, along roadways, and in empty lots. The plants have large, oval leaves and tall, straight stems. If you break a milkweed stem, sticky, white juice oozes out. It looks like milk, which is how these plants got their name.

You will also find insects and other animals wherever milkweed grows. The plants and the animals all belong to a small **ecosystem**. An ecosystem is like a little town, made up of living and nonliving things. Each member of the ecosystem has a special role to play in the community. They all depend on one another to **survive**.

Milkweed got its name from the white liquid contained in the stem. The liquid can hurt your eyes, so don't rub your eyes after touching milkweed.

Spring in a Milkweed Patch

Milkweed stems and leaves die each winter. New milkweed plants grow when warm, spring weather comes. Some of the new plants **sprout** from seeds that have been lying on the ground all winter. A tiny root grows down from the seed into the ground. A tiny shoot grows up.

Other new milkweed plants grow from the roots of last year's plants. The roots stay alive through the winter. They form long **runners** just under the ground, with many plants growing up from them. The runners keep growing longer, so the milkweed patch becomes a little larger each year.

Left: *This tiny shoot has sprouted from a seed.* Right: *These plants are still very small. Full-grown milkweed plants can be as many as 4 feet (1 m) high.*

Common milkweed has pink or purple flowers. This flower is just about to open.

Milkweed plants that grow from seeds begin as tiny shoots.

9

Milkweed Flowers

By summer, the milkweed plants are from 3 to 4 feet (91–122 cm) tall. They are ready to bloom. In most places in North America, common milkweed blooms from late June to August. The plants carry dozens of tiny, pink flowers that grow in bunches. Each bunch looks like one big flower, but it is really many small flowers.

The flowers of milkweed give off a heavy scent. Most people don't care for the scent of milkweed flowers. Bees and butterflies are drawn to the smell, though. They come to the milkweed flowers to feed on **nectar**, a sweet liquid in the center of the flowers. A milkweed patch is an important source of food for these insects.

Milkweed plants bloom in the summer. Inset: *The plants have many flowers, but only a few of the flowers will produce seeds.*

11

Insect Visitors

Insects that come to drink nectar from milkweed flowers also help the plants to make seeds. They take **pollen** from one flower to another. Pollen is a powder made by the male part of the flower. The milkweed stores its pollen in tiny **sacs**. The sacs are joined in pairs so that they form little *V*'s. When an insect visits a flower, its legs brush over the pollen sacs. The sacs are caught on the insect's legs.

The insect carries the pollen sacs along as it flies to another milkweed flower. The center of each flower has a little trap that catches the pollen sacs and pulls them from the insect. In this way pollen from one flower reaches the **pistil**, or the female part, of another flower. Then seeds begin to form.

Honeybees carry the milkweed's pollen sacs with them to the next plant they visit. Inset: Honeybees visit a milkweed plant to eat nectar.

The milkweed plant is
pretty but poisonous to
humans and animals.
For this reason,
farmers don't want it
on their land.

14

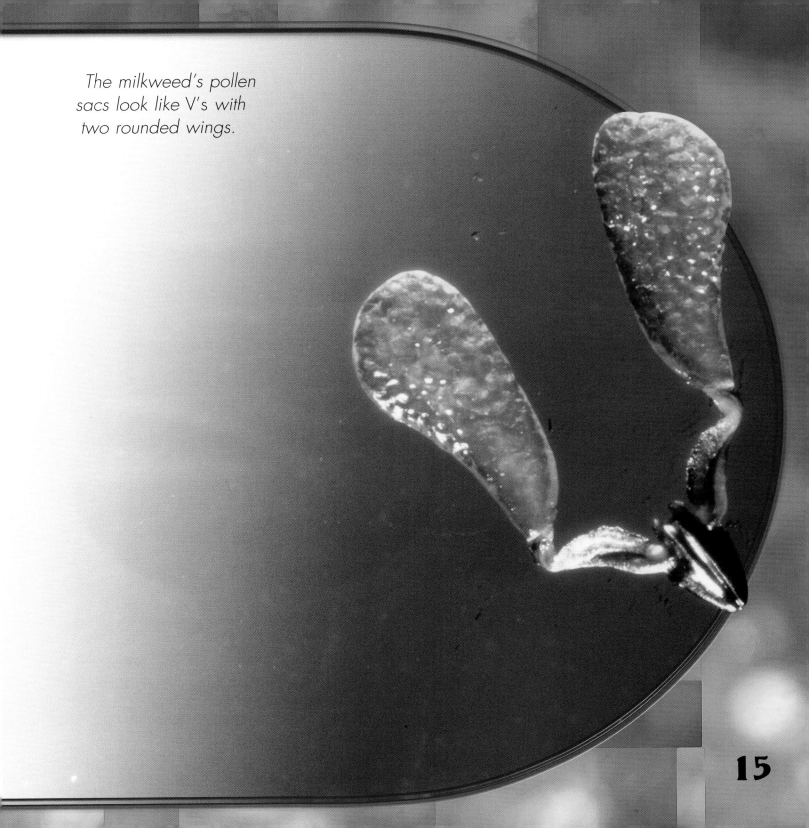

The milkweed's pollen sacs look like V's with two rounded wings.

15

Monarchs and Milkweed

Monarch butterflies depend on milkweed in many ways. Monarchs feed on milkweed nectar, and female monarchs lay their eggs on milkweed leaves. The eggs hatch from four to five days later. Monarch caterpillars crawl out and begin to eat the leaves. They grow quickly. After about three weeks, the caterpillar becomes a **pupa**. It fastens itself to a leaf and forms a hard case around its body. Inside, over several weeks, the pupa changes into a butterfly. Finally the butterfly crawls out and spreads its wings.

The monarch's bright colors are a warning to birds that eat insects. Monarchs taste like milkweed, because milkweed is their only food. Milkweed tastes terrible, and its white juice is poisonous to some animals. Birds don't bother monarchs and their caterpillars.

Top: *A monarch egg.* Inset Left: *Monarch caterpillars are striped.* Bottom: *A monarch pupa.* Inset Right: *An adult monarch crawls out of its case.*

More Milkweed Eaters

Monarch caterpillars are not the only insects that dine on milkweed plants. Milkweed bugs eat the seeds of the plants. Milkweed beetles eat the leaves. The young, or **larvae**, of the beetles live underground. They feed on milkweed roots. The adult bugs and beetles are colored orange and black, as are monarch butterflies. Their bright colors tell birds and other **predators** to stay away.

Tiny, green **aphids** are often found on milkweed leaves. The aphids suck juices from the plants. The little, red **mite** is another juice sucker. A milkweed patch is a source of food for all these creatures.

As do monarch butterflies, milkweed beetles taste bitter to predators. Inset: Aphids feed on the milky white liquid produced by the milkweed plant.

Mites are very small. Some are no bigger than the period at the end of this sentence. This mite is about the size of this letter o.

Below: Milkweed bugs feed on the seeds of milkweed plants.

20

It takes a monarch pupa a little more than a month to change into an adult butterfly. During that time, the insect stays inside a hard case.

The adult monarch's bright colors are a warning. The colors tell predators that the monarch tastes bitter, as does milkweed.

21

Ladybugs and Ants

Other insects come to a milkweed patch in search of the aphids that feed there. Some of these insects are predators. Aphids are the favorite food of ladybug beetles and their larvae. The ladybugs help to keep the number of aphids down, so that aphids do not eat up all the milkweed.

Ants look for aphids in a milkweed patch, too. Ants do not eat aphids. Instead, some ants keep herds of aphids. Aphids make a sweet substance called **honeydew**, which the ants love to eat. The ants catch aphids and tend to them the way humans do with cows. The ants put the aphids out to feed on the milkweed, and then the ants collect the honeydew that the aphids make.

Aphids are about the same size as the head of a pin, so it is easy for ants to round them up and to keep them under control.

Hunters and Trappers

With so many insects living and feeding in it, a milkweed patch is a great hunting ground for spiders. Many spiders trap insects in webs of silk, which the spiders produce from inside their bodies. The jumping spider does not spin a web. It prowls around the milkweed plant looking for insects. When it sees one, it leaps out and bites the insect. The spider's bite is poisonous, and the insect stops moving. Then the spider eats the insect.

Crab spiders hide among the milkweed flowers. A crab spider looks almost like a flower in the bunch. It waits quietly until an insect comes to drink nectar. Then it pounces on its **prey** and bites it.

A female jumping spider lays her eggs on a milkweed leaf. She wraps the eggs in a case made of silk that her body produces.

Ladybug larvae feed on aphids. If there were too many aphids in the milkweed patch, the plants would die.

The crab spider hides among the milkweed flowers. When a honeybee comes to the flowers in search of nectar, the crab spider catches the bee.

This jumping spider has caught a fly on a milkweed leaf.

27

Fall in a Milkweed Patch

By fall the milkweed plants have formed seedpods. The fat, bumpy pods are up to 4 inches (10 cm) long. Inside, hundreds of flat, brown seeds are packed closely together. Each seed has its own **parachute** of fine, silky hairs. When the seedpods open, the parachutes unfold. They catch the wind, and the seeds float away through the air.

Birds eat many milkweed seeds, but other seeds survive and sprout in the spring. Wherever seeds land, a new milkweed patch can grow.

Milkweed seedpods grow in pairs. Inset Left: *Milkweed seeds are light enough to float.* Inset Right: *These seeds are bursting out of the pod.*

The Milkweed Patch Community

The plants and the animals of the milkweed patch need one another in many ways. Milkweed plants need the help of insects to make seeds. Insects get food from the milkweed plants. Some of these insects become food for spiders and other predators. Predators keep the number of insects from growing too large, so that insects do not eat up all the milkweed plants. For the monarch butterfly and some other insects, a milkweed patch is a nursery where the young grow into adults. Nonliving things are important to the milkweed patch, too. These plants need sunlight, water, and good soil to grow.

A milkweed patch is just one of the many ecosystems on Earth. In each of these communities, living things depend on each other and on their surroundings.

Glossary

aphids (AY-fidz) Tiny insects that feed by sucking juices from plants.

ecosystem (EE-koh-sis-tem) A community of living things and the surroundings, such as air, soil, and water, in which they live.

honeydew (HUH-nee-doo) A sweet substance produced by aphids.

larvae (LAHR-vee) The plural form of larva, the early life stage of certain animals that differs greatly from the adult stage.

mite (MYT) A tiny member of the spider family.

nectar (NEK-tur) A sweet liquid made in the center of a flower.

parachute (PAYR-uh-shoot) A milkweed seed's silky attachment, which catches the wind.

pistil (PIS-tuhl) The female part of a flower.

pollen (PAH-lin) A powder made by the male parts of flowers.

predators (PREH-duh-terz) Animals that catch and eat other animals for food.

prey (PRAY) An animal that is hunted by another animal for food.

pupa (PYOO-pah) The second stage of life for an insect, in which it changes from a larva to an adult.

runners (RUH-nerz) Long, thin roots that lie just under the surface of the ground.

sacs (SAKS) Small pouches.

sprout (SPROWT) To begin to grow.

survive (sur-VYV) To stay alive.

Index

Web Sites

Due to the changing nature of Internet links, PowerKids Press has developed an online list of Web sites related to the subject of this book. This site is updated regularly. Please use this link to access the list:
www.powerkidslinks.com/lse/milkweco/